The Song in My Head

Justin Conigliaro

Illustrator: Joseph Kindya (owner and tattooer of Brooklyn Ink Tattoo since 2005)
Production Artist: Adam Kokoni

Print information available on the last page

Rev. date: 05/08/2019

To order additional copies of this book, contact:
Xlibris
1-888-795-4274
www.Xlibris.com
Orders@Xlibris.com

The Song in My Head

Illustrated by Joseph Kindya

There's a song in my head that I sing everyday because it says

all the words I've been wanting to say.

It says thank you, I'm sorry and I'm here for you. It says I know that the words that you tell me are true.

The song makes me brave as the words leave my mouth

because I've never been sure how to say them myself.

I sing to spaghetti when its tangled and twirled, I sing to the prettiest girl in the world.

I sing from my roof when I want to be heard, I sing it so loud and I sing every word.

I sing to my dog when we walk around town, I sing to myself when there's no one around.

I sing to the songs that have helped me to say anything that I want, anytime of the day.

I sing to the clouds and I sing to the birds and as long as there's music I'll always have words.

It's always so hard not to speak at my best, so I sing to get all

the words off my chest.

Beautifully helpful beginning to end, the song in my head is forever my friend.

Printed in the United States
By Bookmasters